Jim Henson's Doodle Dreams

Meredith® Books
Des Moines, Iowa

Contributing Editor: Don Curry
Contributing Designer: Chad Jewell

Meredith Books
1716 Locust Street
Des Moines, Iowa 50309-3023
www.meredithbooks.com

First Edition.

Printed in the United States of America.
Library of Congress Control Number: 2008923673
ISBN: 978-0-696-23988-5

I know that I personally have felt quite happy
because I've done what I wanted to do.
I pursued my interests and have thus managed
to combine my business with lots of fun.
I guess my only advice is to do what you enjoy,
and try to do your best with it.

Jim Henson

Introduction By Jim Lewis

JIM HENSON'S CAREER BEGAN AROUND 1955 WITH a local Washington, D.C., television show called *Sam and Friends*. I was born in 1955.

That's pretty much where the similarities end. By 1984, when I actually met Jim Henson, he was already recognized as a visionary, a television pioneer, and a remarkably versatile artist and performer. I, on the other hand, was still a struggling writer, only vaguely recognized by my family in Boonton, New Jersey.

And yet Jim Henson saw something he liked about my talents and gave me a chance. Jim gave me—and every other person who worked with him—an opportunity to explore our strangest ideas and create whatever quirky silliness we might be able to conjure. By believing in us he made us believe in ourselves.

Jim Henson also led by example—creating, enhancing, and getting excited about new ideas. And when he expressed his own ideas, he usually did so in the way that came most naturally to him—through his artwork. With everything else that Jim accomplished, it is easy to forget that he began his career as a visual artist—using art to express ideas and emotions and to make us appreciate each other and our world.

This book is a celebration of Jim Henson and his art, of the way he expressed himself in his most creative and contemplative moments. It is also a chance for Jim's art to inspire all of us once again. As for the words, they are my attempts to capture Jim's spirit. It is a spirit that I believe lives on—not only among those who had the privilege of knowing and working with Jim Henson but in every person whose life his work continues to touch.

Jim Henson, 1969

Jim Henson

JIM HENSON WAS AN EXTRAORDINARY artist who invented unique worlds and characters that remain as original and alive today as when they were created.

Born September 24, 1936, in Mississippi, Jim pursued his interest in art throughout his school years. In 1954, while still in high school, Jim began performing puppets on a local Saturday morning program in Washington, D.C. The following year, as a freshman at the University of Maryland, he launched his own twice-daily five-minute show, *Sam and Friends*. There—along with his assistant, fellow University of Maryland student and future wife Jane Nebel—Jim introduced many mainstays that would become his trademark: music, inspired silliness, and innovative technical tricks. Local success led to guest appearances on national television programs such as *The Steve Allen Show* and *The Ed Sullivan Show* as well as several television specials.

In 1969 Jim created a family of characters—including Ernie and Bert, Oscar the Grouch, Grover, Cookie Monster, and Big Bird—for *Sesame Street*, which continues to entertain and educate today, almost 40 years later. In 1975 Jim launched *The Muppet Show*, an international hit. This naturally led to Hollywood, where the Muppets have now starred in six feature films, including the classic family favorite *The Muppet Movie*.

During the 1980s Jim also brought two original fantasy films to the big screen, *The Dark Crystal* and *Labyrinth*. The multitalented staff that helped bring these films to life became what is now known as Jim Henson's Creature Shop, which continues to set industry standards in puppetry, animatronics, performance, and performance technology. Jim also created memorable awardwinning television series and specials, including *Jim Henson's Muppet Babies*, *Jim Henson's The Storyteller*, and the world's first multination television coproduction, *Fraggle Rock*.

On May 16, 1990, Jim Henson died in New York City at the age of 53. But with his keen ability for drawing together a diverse team of performers, artists, and collaborators who shared his vision and creativity, Jim ensured that his work and creative vision live on.

Be interested in everything.

An open mind is a good place to start.

Stay open to everything. The more that you see, hear, and experience, the more connections you'll make.

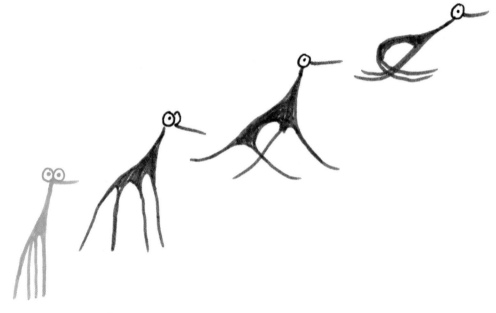

Beginning is the
hardest thing.

CREATIVITY.

Taking something enormously strange
and somehow making it strangely familiar.

Try to keep enough balls in the air so that when some fall onto the ground, you've got others up there.

You have to remember: Problems can be solved. There *is* something you can do.

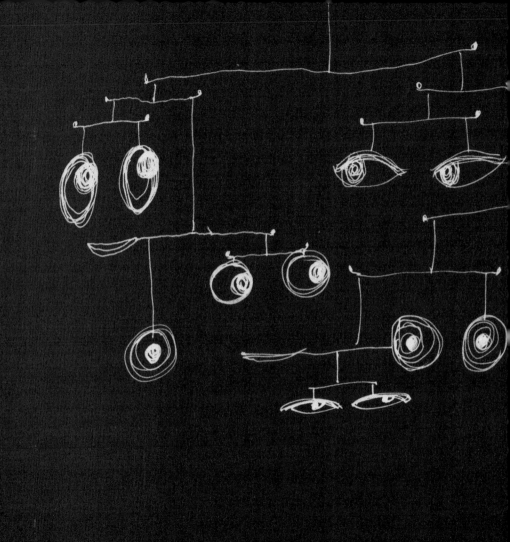

Every once in a while,
stop and look around. It doesn't
matter where you are; there's usually
something right there in front of you
that will surprise and inspire you.

If you're open to them,
great ideas are everywhere.

Being afraid isn't always a bad thing. Sometimes you need that trembling feeling to remind you how exciting it is to be doing something new.

When you take chances, you're going to fail. That's inevitable. You can either let failure turn you away from your dream or inspire you to dream bigger.

Understanding other points of view keeps you fresh. You can look at the same thing one way forever, and it never seems to change. Then someone comes in and turns it upside down or inside out and suddenly, together, you've made something amazing.

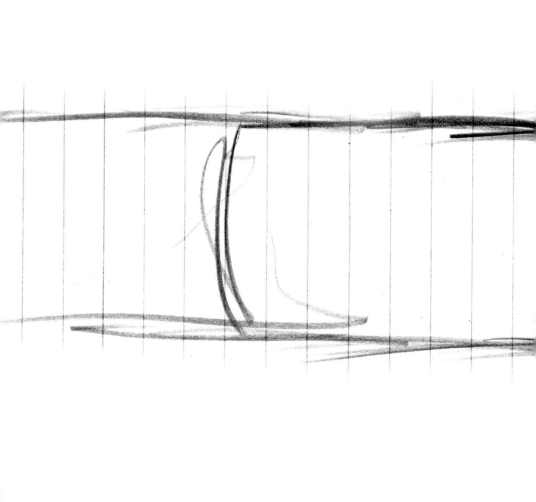

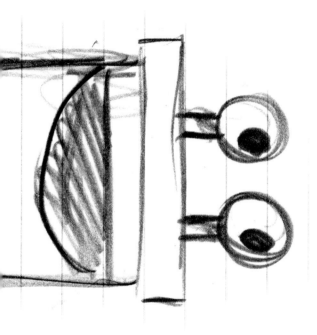

Try to instigate silliness.

It's helpful to be focused, but don't let that crowd new ideas out of your head.

If you worry too much about the way things are supposed to be, you're a lot more likely to end up following the crowd.

You are where you are because that's where you need to be. And if you need to move on, you'll move on.

A sense of wonder is the most incredible gift you can share.

When you stay positive,
it's harder for other people
to be negative . . .

and that can only be
a good thing.

If you approach the world with wide eyes, an open mind, and a willingness to take a chance, you'll likely surprise yourself.

You can be a better leader if you're not shouting all the time. Shouting only makes people cover their ears, and pretty soon nobody is listening.

*If you find a place where
people look happy, stick around ...
and invite some friends.*

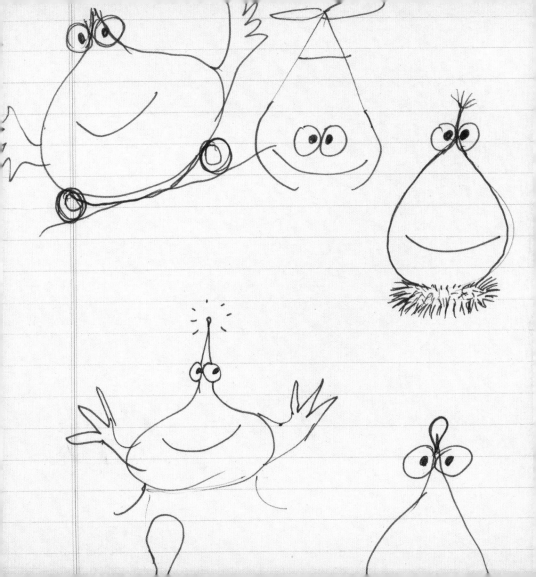

Do things.
Do them well.
Then, right away, do
something totally different
and do it even better.

It's good to have big goals that seem impossible and huge—like saving the world and helping mankind.

Even if you don't reach those goals, it's great to start your day headed in that general direction.

Silly is good!
It's worth pursuing.

When something you create
comes alive, that's magic.

*Stuff like that is
impossible to explain.*

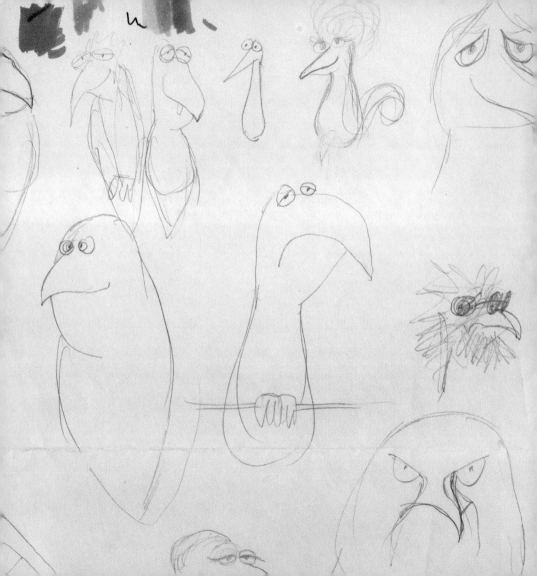

Some of us birds are made to fly,
To flap our wings and reach up to the sky,
And soar around so gracefully
That all the world looks up to see
And say: "How do they fly?"
Oh me! Oh my!

Be curious. If you're always wondering what's going to happen next, you'll never lose your passion.

Go outside and look
up at a tree. Better
yet, look at one leaf.
It's just so perfect.
Everything we do
falls short of that.
But that's OK.
Being awestruck is a
good thing.

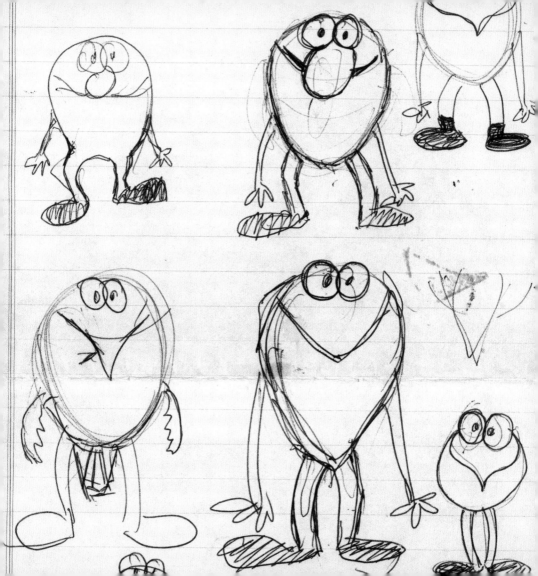

If you take who you are and work with it over and over again, there's a pretty good chance you'll end up who you want to be.

Enjoy music,
people . . . or just
gazing at the stars.
This is the opposite of
ambition but just as
important. It gives life
balance.

Working together
is like being part of
a wheel. When the
wheel is moving,
you don't see the
individual spokes.

Spark the goodness
in others.

If you listen too
closely to the sound, you
may miss the music.

A good laugh, the kind that just bursts out. You know, the kind that comes from who-knows-where. When it happens, that's the best. HA!

An artist gives people back a part of themselves—the stories and sounds, the feeling of what it's like to be alive.

That's a pretty powerful gift.

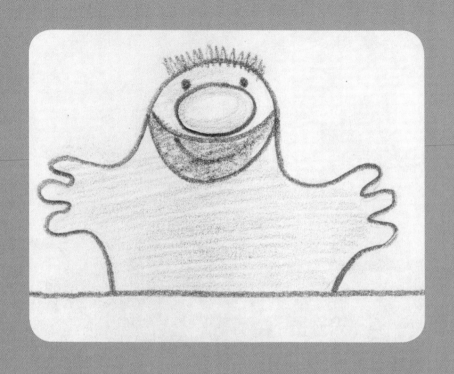

There are many ways of
doing something.

Look for what no one has tried before.
Go back and question one or more of the
basic "givens" of a situation.

It seems that if you want to go anywhere really interesting, you usually have to travel through chaos to get there.

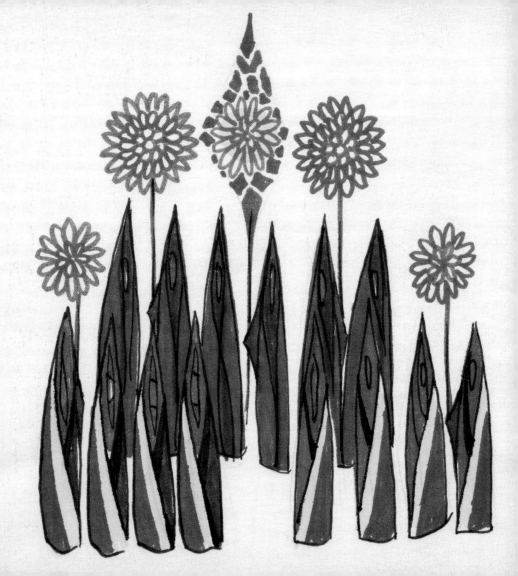

Appreciate the flowers, the
sunlight, the trees.
Take it all in. If you appreciate
life's beauty you discover that
you're surrounded by it.

Working with others is one of life's great joys. You take an idea and together you expand it until it becomes something much bigger than any of you could have done alone.

Art is like magic.

It's something that you practice and practice until you can make something that seems absolutely impossible seem totally natural.

We're all like eggs—fragile and full of possibilities. But unless we come out of our shells, we just stay eggs.

When you say you've come to a conclusion about something, you're only saying you've stopped thinking about it.

Kids think anything is possible.
Be a kid again.

Always do
things you can
be proud of.

It's our duty to encourage those who come after us to appreciate and understand the past.